THE PROCESS OF GOD

Gerald Courtney

The Process of God – Christianity

DEDICATION

This book was written in the memory of my father, Bill Courtney, and is dedicated to God my Father in Heaven for giving me this message to pass on to Christians everywhere.

Contents

INTRODUCTION

God is bringing us to a new era of new wineskins. Any time a new wineskin is made there has to be the death of an animal to produce it. It had to be flexible and expandable for the increase. Oiled to help the flexibility as we need the oil of the Holy Spirit to receive the new era that is coming forth. God cannot put the new wine (the new church structure) into the old wineskin (the old church structure). The old wineskin cannot handle the new wine. New wine will expand and increase as it ferments. Old wineskins are stiff and rigid. It will not accept the change. This book is about the process that God by His Holy Spirit wants us to go through. May God by His Holy Spirit open our eyes and ears to the new thing God is doing on the earth. The status quo must go.

Ephesians 4:13(NASB) sums up the purpose of this book: *"Until we all attain to the unity of the faith, and of the knowledge of the Son of God, to a mature man, to the measure of the stature which belongs to the fullness of Christ"*

8

CHAPTER ONE

REVELATION OF THE PROCESS

In the early 1980s, God gave me a revelation of the process the church would go through in these last days. This was a three-step process. Anytime the Body of Christ goes through a process it means the members individually go through it.

The process comes to each as he is positioned for it. Not all go through it at the same time or at the same speed. The factor that controls how a person goes through the process or how fast depends on one thing: submission to the process.

There are a lot of processes that a Christian can go through if they are to grow in the knowledge of God. Yes, the knowledge of God. The knowledge of God will reveal our destiny and the image that God wants us to see.

Ephesians 1:17-19 (NASB) ...*that the God of our Lord Jesus Christ, the Father of glory, may give to you a spirit of wisdom and of revelation in the knowledge of him. I pray that the eyes of your heart may be enlightened, so that you will know what is the hope of His calling, what are the riches of the glory of His inheritance in the saints, and what is the surpassing greatness of His power toward us who believe. These are in accordance with the working of the strength of His might..."*

The Image He wants for us is as kings and priests.

1 Peter 2:9 (NASB) *"But you are a CHOSEN RACE, a royal PRIESTHOOD, A Holy Nation, a people for God's own possession, so that you may proclaim the excellencies of Him who has called you out of darkness into His marvelous light."*

Revelation 5:10 (NASB) *"And have made us kings and priests to our God; And we shall reign on earth." How we submit to the process of God determines how fast the process accomplishes His purpose.*

Correction, Connection, and Completion

The three steps the church would go through that the Holy Spirit revealed to me were Correction, Connection, and Completion.

This revelation that the Holy Spirit gave me has never left me. This process for the Body of Christ has become a part of me and my own process along with other processes that I have gone through concerning submission and laying down my own will and rights.

Romans 12: 1-2 (AMPC) *"I APPEAL to you therefore, brethren, and beg of you in view of (all) the mercies of God, to make a decisive dedication of your bodies [presenting all your members and faculties] as a living sacrifice, holy (devoted, consecrated) and well-pleasing to God, which is your reasonable (rational, intelligent) service and spiritual worship. Do not be conformed to this world (this age), [fashioned after and adapted to its external, superficial customs], but be transformed (changed) by the [entire] renewal of your mind [by its new ideals and its new attitude], so that you may prove [for yourselves] what is good and acceptable and perfect will of God, even the thing which is good and acceptable and perfect [in His sight for you].*

Each of the three processes flows or overlaps into the next and will blend together. The first two flow and blend before the last of Completion can take place.

Christ said, "I will build my church and the gates of hell will not prevail against it." No matter what the devil does he can not keep Christ from building His Church.

Any building project is a process. Mankind in his religious ways has tried to build the church in his own ways with religious structures. These will have to be and are being corrected by Christ.

This is the era of Correction for the Body of Christ. This new era we are moving into is an era of restoration. These structures of man have been established over the centuries. They have been set up by man's traditions.

Mark 7:13a (KJV) *"Making the word of God of none effect through your tradition"* Mark 7:13a NASB) *"thus invalidation the word of God by your tradition which you have handed down; and you do many things such as that"*

Wow! Can you understand that we have a lot of traditions in the Church today?

Tradition says this: "We already know what God wants to do and how He wants to do it".

One of the main purposes of the Holy Spirit is to bring newness and a fresh wind from God that elevates us into the new place God wants for us. He doesn't try to make the old way new; He gives a new way of living in Christ and Christ in us.

John 16:13 (AMPC) *"But when He, the Spirit of Truth (the Truth-giving Spirit) comes, He will guide you into all the Truth (the whole, full Truth). For He will not speak His own message [on His own authority]; but He will tell whatever He hears [from the Father; He will give the message that has been given to Him], and He will announce and declare to you the things that are to come [that will happen in the future]".*

Believe it or not, we do not have all the truth yet. We can know what God wants to do in the future and we can pull the future into the present. This happens through the process of Correction and being realigned. Realignment doesn't mean a new alignment but to restore the image that was always meant to be.

We see so many denominations and congregations that do not meet the requirements of Ephesians 4:11. This is where Christ ascended and gave the five-fold anointing to the church to equip the saints to do the work of the ministry. We can fool ourselves but without these five gifts from Christ, the equipping of the saints will not be complete.

The church has been out of alignment and has missed the goal of the five gifts or anointing: of Apostles, Prophets, Teachers, Pastors, and Evangelists. The five gifts are needed in order to reposition us so that we may see the full expression of Christ and what He has to do to prepare us for Completion (maturity).

Tradition says we do not need Correction and it leaves little room for proper Connection between members.

There is a 'day of the saints' coming where all saints will work with power and authority fulfilling their destiny and all God has for them to do.

Many Prophets have prophesied this. You can read about it in Bishop Bill Hamon's book *The Day of the Saints*. A true tabernacle will be erected by Christ and not by the traditions of man.

Hebrews 8:2 (AMPC) *"As officiating Priest, a Minister in the holy places and in the true tabernacle which is erected not by man but by the Lord."*

Men have set up their own houses and their own kingdoms. The day of the one-man show is coming to an end and God is correcting this to a plurality of leadership just as it is in heaven. We do not see Connection and relationship coming together in most church structures today. It is just not set up for that and must be corrected by the Holy Spirit by bringing revelation.

If we could see the overall view of the whole Body of Christ, we would see that Correction and Connection are beginning to take place. The body builds up the body.

Ephesians 4:16 (AMPC) *For because of Him the whole body (the church, in all its various parts), closely joined and firmly knit together by the joints and ligaments with which it is supplied, when each part [with power adapted to its need] is working properly [in all its functions], grows to full maturity, building itself up in love."*

The body builds up the body with the equipping by the five-fold gifts, anointing or graces of Christ mentioned in Ephesians 4:11. Each member must find his proper place and function. Until we do this, we as individuals cannot and will not be able to come into our full destiny and all God has for us. The church has in large part missed in helping find where each one has their place and function.

CHAPTER TWO

CORRECTION

Our first step in the process is Correction; it has to come first so we can move into Connection and real relationship.

The flow between Correction and Connection can happen at times as the process proceeds forward. God has no limit and is immeasurable. He is always increasing us toward our destiny.

Ephesians 1:19 (AMPC) *"And [so that you can know and understand] what is the immeasurable and unlimited and surpassing greatness of His power in and for us who believe, as demonstrated in the working of His mighty strength,"*

The process as I have experienced in my life of Correction is three-fold. As we know, the Father corrects His sons that He loves.

Hebrews 12:5b (AMPC) says *"My son, do not think lightly or scorn to submit to the Correction and discipline of the Lord, nor lose courage and give up and faint when you are reproved or corrected by Him;*

Realignment

The first step that unfolds in Correction is realignment. Realign means "align again or to position us again." We could say realigning means to set in order. To take that which is out of place or order and put it back into its right place or order so it might function rightly. This is what happens every time the Holy Spirit renews our mind and begins to transform us as mentioned in Romans 12:2. As we study this further we can see we begin to receive a new image of ourselves and Christ, and begin to be repositioned with new patterns, attitudes in the way we live. That means we must submit our faculties, abilities, and power to the Holy Spirit.

The church and individuals in many ways have gotten out of position as mentioned in Mark 7:13 they have nullified and made the word of God of no effect by their traditions or the structures they have set up. God is beginning to change and correct this. Traditions have set up structures and walls that are not the structure, or you could say the building, house, or body that Christ wants to build. In some cases, Christ by the Holy Spirit will have to tear down or root up the old wineskin structures.

This is one reason He is bringing forth the five-fold ascension gifts from Ephesians 4:11. They will be part of rooting up as in:

Jeremiah 1:10 (NASB) *"See, I have appointed you this day over the nations and over the kingdoms, To pluck up and to break down, To destroy and to overthrow, To build and to plant."*

He must realign or reposition His Church and the individuals in it.

When NASA launches a rocket to the moon or anywhere, they keep looking at the position of the rocket relative to its destination. Or you could say its destiny. Their exact word if it's off course is that they must change its attitude. It needs a new attitude.

Attitude: A position assumed of a specific purpose.

You could say we need a new pattern or patterns in our life. Our attitude is the position we take toward anything.

This is what Romans 12:2 in the Amplified Bible says:

"Do not be conformed to this world (this age), [fashioned after and adapted to its external, superficial customs], but be transformed (changed) by the [entire] renewal of your mind [by its new ideals and its new attitude], so that you may prove [for your selves] what is the good and acceptable and perfect [in His sight for you]."

When our minds are renewed by the Holy Spirit we receive new ideals and new attitudes. New ideals mean that we receive new goals and new images of ourselves. New attitudes mean we have been repositioned, and we have new patterns in our life. A paradigm shift in our life is needed. We all need this shift continually.

The Holy Spirit is constantly doing this day by day to form us into the image of Christ. The Holy Spirit's very nature is to create that which is new and bring freshness and newness to the body of Christ continually and to all of us individually. He is always increasing us.

Slowly God's presence and power are being removed from the old structures and the mindsets that tradition has set up. Where glory has dwelt because of grace, it is now beginning to diminish. Traditions of men say we already know what God wants to do and how He wants to do it. They set up programs and forms. I have witnessed the program being more important than what the Holy Spirit wants to do.

The first step in Correction and moving to the new is being willing to leave the old. God help us! Only the Holy Spirit can bring that revelation to us and change us. We have to get past the attitude or position of; that is the way it has always been done, and we have all the truth, and we already know what God wants to do. I repent of this.

The old structures are not always set up to see His sheep be fed and equipped and activated to do the work of the ministry. I was talking to a man one day that was saying he was not seeing anything happening in his church. Before I knew it and not even thinking, out of my mouth came these words: "God never intended His sheep to stay in a pasture that they are not being fed" Christ gave us a pattern to follow as did the early Church. It has always been amazing to me that we do not follow the pattern as the early Church and what Christ did.

There must be Correction and change. No growth will come without Correction and change. Jesus' pattern and the pattern of the early church changed men into five-fold ascension gifts, anointings and set the world on fire. And to this day it affects us.

What is the hindrance and the resistance today? Is it that we are not aligned with that pattern and must be realigned? The structure that is set up must be adjusted, and in some cases, torn down and rebuilt. It has been the old wineskins and old structures of the traditions of men that make His word of no effect.

His word creates and changes us if it can get to us. Our traditions put a ceiling over our heads that prevents us from the revelation word of God getting to us. We must realign ourselves and be willing to change the patterns that we have set up in the Church and in our lives.

Refinement

As I am moving through this process, I begin to realize that the first step of Correction, of being realigned or repositioned with new patterns of my life, brings me into the next step of Correction which is to be REFINED. Correction always starts with repentance. Yes, all Christians need to repent continually so that their mind and direction is changed.

REFINED: Freed from impurities. The key to open the door to any process God might have us to go through is submission. If there is no submission, then there is no remission. Remission: pardon; forgiveness, as of sins or offenses.

Sin is defined as missing the mark. Missing God's mark, goal or will for our life. We can have forgiveness through repentance and the confessing of our sins. It is so important that we find those blind areas, those hidden faults or sins that need repentance.

King David said this in Psalms 19:12(NASB) *"Who can discern his errors? Acquit me of hidden faults."*

Repentance literally means to change our mind and turn around from the direction we are going. You could say we change our position or attitude.

Is the Church missing the mark in many areas?

We must go through the process of Correction. Will we be willing to submit and leave the old? We must be realigned first then God can, by His Holy Spirit, refine us.

Psalms 66:10(AMPC) *"for you, O God, have probed us; You have tried us as silver is tried, refined, and purified."*

Revelation 3:14-20 (NASB) *"to the angel of the church in Laodicea write: These are the words of the Amen, the faithful and true witness, the ruler of God's creation. I know your deed, that you are neither cold nor hot. I wish you were either one or the other! So, because you are lukewarm - neither hot nor cold - I am about to spit you out of my mouth. You say, "I am rich; I have acquired wealth and do not need a thing." But you do not realize that you are wretched, pitiful, poor, blind and naked. I counsel you to buy from me gold reined in the fire, so you can become rich; and white clothes to wear, so you can cover your shameful nakedness; and salve to put on your eyes, so you can see. Those whom I love I rebuke and discipline. So be earnest and repent. Here I am! I stand at the door and knock. If anyone hears my voice and opens the door, I will come in and eat with that person, and they with me."*

Here he speaks to one of seven churches. He tells them all one thing in common. Let's look at verse 22. *"Whoever has ears, let them hear what the Spirit says to the churches."* In these verses, He is telling us we must repent, change our mind and our attitude or position we have taken, mostly because of traditions that have been handed down to us through religious formalities.

The day of the one-man show is coming to a close. A plurality of leadership is the way God acts. God the Father, God the Son, and God the Holy Spirit. That is a plurality. Christ ascended and gave us a plurality of leadership, five of them in Ephesians 4:11 (NIV): *"So Christ himself gave the apostles, the prophets, the evangelists, the pastors and teachers..."*

*

Take a look at Ephesians 2:19-20 (NIV): *"Consequently, you are no longer foreigners and strangers, but fellow citizens with God's people and also members of his household, Built on the foundation of the apostles and prophets, with Jesus himself as the chief cornerstone."*

I heard a very righteous Christian man say that he looked at this verse in Ephesians 2 as for the apostles and prophets as in Bible days. If it says this then, it nullifies the ascension gifts that Christ gave in Ephesians 4:11. That is just what tradition will do to us. In that case, it made the word of God of no effect to that man.

The status quo is coming to an end and God is releasing a new era. God is bringing Correction at this hour to the Body of Christ. He is realigning us first, and then He is able to refine us and remove the impurities.

There are many other scriptures that talk about the Correction, discipline, and refinement that God has for us to bring us to the full nature of Christ. We do not have it all yet.

When gold is purified, and many scriptures say our refinement is like that, it is heated up until the impurities jump out of the gold and leave it pure in order that it can be used.

We are not pure yet and do not have it all together, but we want to act as if we do. I repent. That is exactly what God does with His Church and us individually. As I prayed for God to remove some things, and I am sure I still have some that are hidden, these things begin to manifest and come to the surface. I told the Holy Spirit that I do not want those things. I do not want to be like that. I asked why is this happening? He showed me that I had prayed for them to be removed, and He was bringing them to the surface to expose them so they could be removed. He was refining me.

I first had to reposition myself through submission for him to be able to do this. Even as I started writing this paper, the Holy Spirit has had me in His presence showing me things about myself that needed to be corrected. It was like a light bulb going off. I had no desire to correct these things before He showed me. Praise the Lord and the Holy Spirit that God loves us so much and wants to see us reach our destiny.

Decision Decides Destiny

I have what I call the triple D's. Decision Decides Destiny.

I have found that decision has to be mixed with desire. The prayer that made the biggest difference in my life and when I was at my lowest point was "God help me change my desire".

We can have decision mixed with desire but we also need persistence to show us the way. Here is a passage from scripture that talks about persistence and gives us some clues on how to reach our destiny:

Luke 11:5-10 (NASB) *Then He said to them, "Suppose one of you has a friend, and goes to him at midnight and says to him, 'Friend, lend me three loaves; for a friend of mine has come to me from a journey, and I have nothing to set before him'; and from inside he answers and says, 'Do not bother me; the door has already been shut and my children and I are in bed; I cannot get up and give you anything.' I tell you, even though he will not get up and give him anything because he is his friend, yet because of his persistence he will get up and give him as much as he needs.*

"So I say to you, ask, and it will be given to you; seek, and you will find; knock, and it will be opened to you. For everyone who asks, receives; and he who seeks, finds; and to him who knocks, it will be opened.

The analogy that I received from the Holy Spirit in bringing things to the surface so He could remove them was as follows: It is like a river that comes to a turbulent rapid. When it gets to the rapids, everything up to that point is on the bottom and is hidden, and has not been disturbed, but when it hits the turbulent rapids, that which is hidden and on the bottom is stirred up and comes to the surface.

Many times disturbances, or can we say the fire, are allowed to come into our lives that it might bring some things to the surface so they might be removed. We must submit to the fire. The three Hebrew men were thrown in the fire, yet they were not alone. There was a fourth One there in the fire, and it was the Son of God.

Many times I have had to bring good and bad things to the Holy Spirit. I had to bring all God had given me, all that He had promised me, and lay it on the altar and say, "God I give them back. Burn up what is not supposed to be in me and let remain that which I should have." It is all His. I am all in.

I look at Abraham. God gave him the promise of a son and a future destiny. He gave him Isaac, and He required that he bring Isaac and sacrifice him back to Him. Abraham counted his son and the promise as dead, but said God gave him the promise and even if it dies, He is able to resurrect it again. Wow, what faith!

No wonder he was called a friend of God. I want to be a friend of God and the Holy Spirit. I like to call the Holy Spirit my buddy and for Him to come along with me each day. I want to give it all back to God, and let Him resurrect what He wants in my life.

He loves to resurrect that which is dead and make it alive and give it new life again, a resurrection power-filled life!

Luke 9:24 (NASB) *"For whoever wishes to save his life will lose it, but whoever loses his life for My sake, he is the one who will save it."*

Paul knew this process well. He said in Philippians. 3:12(AMP) *"Not that I have already obtained it [this goal of being Christlike] or have already been made perfect, I actively press on so that I may lay hold of that [perfection] for which Christ Jesus took hold of me and made me His own Brethren, I do not regard myself as having laid hold of it yet; but one thing I do: forgetting what lies behind and reaching forward to what lies ahead."*

Wow, what a passage! What a revelation!

Paul knew that God was always bringing him to a higher place. He knew to get there he had to forget that which was behind him. He knew the old attitude or old position was not good enough anymore, that God had a better place, a larger and deeper place. He was bringing him to that higher place, and the only way to get there was to lay down the old and reach in the future for the new.

We must submit to the new and leave the old behind. The old structures, old ways of doing things that contain no power must go. They say doing the same thing and expecting a different result is insanity. Has the church, and we as individuals, been insane or can we say we have the wrong mind? Are we satisfied with the status quo and believe this is the way we have always done things and it is good enough?

The Status Quo Must Go

God forbid! The status quo must go. We need that new mind that only the Holy Spirit gives with the new attitude and position. The first step is being willing to leave the old. Why do the Church and individuals do not want to leave the old? Because they say the old is better.

I have heard many in my day say we want the old-time religion or what revival we had back then.

Luke 5:37-39 (NASB) *"And no one puts new wine into old wineskins; otherwise the new wine will burst the skins and it will be spilled out, and the skins will be ruined. But new wine must be put into fresh new wineskins. And no one, after drinking old wine wishes for the new; for he says, "The old is good enough."*

Again what does tradition say? It says we already know what God wants to do and how He wants to do it. We have the old and it's good enough.

We have to leave the old and press forward to that which is ahead. We have not arrived. We cannot have an escape mentality and say we have arrived and have attained and have all we need until Jesus returns. Paul said they did not do this. We must occupy and possess the Kingdom of God. We must submit to the process. *"Thy will be done on earth as it is in heaven."* We must begin to let Christ build His Church, structure, house, and body. Letting the fullness of Christ be formed in us. Letting Him tear down old traditional man-made structures and mindsets is absolutely necessary. The body needs to build the body, and the five-fold ascension offices, anointings or graces that Christ gave to the Church have to be set in places and begin to function. This must happen in order to see the saints equipped to do the work of the ministry and the body become a full-grown man.

Relationships are key. Relationships are where the body has joints.

Ephesians 4:16 (AMP) *"From Him the whole body [the church, in all its various parts], joined and knitted firmly together by what every joint supplies, when each part is working properly, causes the body to grow and mature, building itself up in [unselfish love]"*

Each person has to find where he fits and what his function is. Without that, we will never come into our true destiny.

DDD = Decision, Decides, Destiny.

It is submission or no remission. We have to be willing to repent and turn toward the new things of God that He wants to bring us into. He is King and we are in His Kingdom. We must be willing to be realigned (repositioned) so we can be refined in order that we can move into the last step of Correction, which is to be redesigned, made into that new image, that new house, structure, or body of Christ. Realigned to be refined.

Redesigned

Ephesians 5:27 (NASB) *"That He might present to Himself the church in all her glory, having no spot or wrinkle or any such thing; but that she would be holy and blameless."*

The redesign for me comes through Jeremiah 1:5 (version) *"Before I formed you in the womb I knew you, and before you were born I consecrated you; I have appointed you a prophet to the nations."*

He knew us and our destiny before we were ever born. He had a design for us. Tradition and man-made religion have formed the wrong design in many ways, with wrong mindsets. God must bring us to a place that we are redesigned and the image that he wants is brought forth. Is. 53:6 (NASB) "All of us like sheep have gone astray, Each of us has turned to his own way: But the LORD has caused the iniquity of us all to fall on Him." A former mentor told me once, that the thing that we had to fear most was that God would let us have our own way. Where the Lord's glory has previously rested and His power has previously manifested because of His grace, it is now slowly being removed. He is beginning to peel off the old layer of wineskins and revealing the new wineskins. For them to make a new wineskin an animal had to die so they could use its skin. Something has to die to have the new wineskin and the new wine. The new wine is the blood of Christ and new life in Him again and again. I just read in Charisma magazine that many or being told to close down conferences that have been going on for years and get back to the basics and coming, closer to Him. We need to turn away from our ways of religious tradition. The Church in many places has a form of Godliness but denies the power thereof. There are Churches that are almost dead with little of the Spirit of God moving.

I recently heard a great apostle say "If that is where you are, leave it now."

Too often we find that there are no relationships between the five-fold offices or graces, much less joints between members where true life flows. The body in most places sits in a pew and never is activated or equipped to the work of the ministry. WHY?

Hebrews 13:21 (AMPC) *"Strengthen (complete, perfect) and make you what you ought to be and equip you with everything good that you may carry out His will; [while He Himself] works in you and accomplishes that which is pleasing in His sight."*

Is this not our goal? The structures are wrong and set up for one-man shows that do not want to be threatened by a plurality of leadership. He wants to redesign us.

Romans 12:2 (AMPC) *"Do not be conformed to this world (this age); [fashioned after and adapted to its external, superficial customs], but be transformed (changed) by the [entire] renewal of your mind [by its new ideal and its new attitude], so that you may prove [for yourselves} what is the good and acceptable and perfect will of God, even the thing which is good and acceptable [in His sight for you].* "

When the Holy Spirit renews our mind, He gives us new ideals. This means a new imagination or a new image of ourselves and who He is. It also means to see more. It raises us to a higher standard of ourselves. He also gives us a new attitude. That means He raises us to a new position. Our destiny is ahead of us. He is always wanting to increase us and draw us closer to Him. It is all about relationship. The Holy Spirit makes our minds new again and again. One of His main functions is to bring us to a new place in God. Our battlefield is in the mind. That is where we are always doing battle. The Holy Spirit can help us have that sound mind.

2 Timothy 1:7 (AMPC version) *"For God did not give us a spirit of timidity (of cowardice, of craven and cringing and fawning fear), but [He has given us a spirit] of power and of love and of calm and well-balanced mind and discipline and self-control."*

As Prophet Kim Clement said, "I am somewhere in the future and I look a lot better than I do right now" We have to learn to pull our destiny from the future into the present. The Holy Spirit through renewing our mind, help us redesign ourselves and do this. Paul said "I reach towards what is ahead"

Revelation 3:20(NASB) *"Behold, I stand at the door and knock; if anyone hears and listens to and heeds My voice and opens the door, I will come in and dine with him."*

That means He spreads a table before us. Let us not settle for crumbs. One thing I have learned is if Jesus dines with me, I begin to have fellowship with Him and gain knowledge of who He really is. It always gives me a better revelation of who I am and who He is. Fellowship means to have a common life with Christ. It gives me a better image of who I am and who I will be. It always brings adjustment to me or Correction and begins to redesign me.

I think of a dream that a good brother revealed to me for interpretation. He said he saw himself as three different images in this dream. One was the way he was as in his image at work in his job. One was dressed up as if he was playing music in a secular band and this final image was dressed as God saw him. The interpretation was simply that God by his Holy Spirit was wanting to bring him into a new design of himself or redesign him or we could say change his image. Along with this came adjustment and Correction. He has begun this process and some Corrections and adjustments have taken place. He even said the other day his wife and others have seen a difference. His image of himself has changed.

Jesus wants us to hear His voice and open the door so He can begin to reveal Himself to us which reveals us to ourselves. It is amazing right after Revelation 3:20 John says this in Revelation 4:1 (AMPC) *"After this I looked, and behold, a door standing open in heaven! And the first voice which I had heard addressing me like [the calling of] a war trumpet said, Come up here, and I will show you what must take place in the future."*

We can open doors to our destiny. DDD. Decision Decides Destiny. Desperation or persistence shows us the way. Seek and keep seeking.

We have choices about which doors we open. I want to forget what is behind and press toward what is ahead and to the higher, upward calling of Christ. I am willing to leave the old. I am willing to open the door of my destiny which is in the future but has always been there even before I was born. We can see our destiny in the future and begin to pull it into the present. I believe this a year of breakthrough into an increase of more of God and His increase in our lives. I believe every year is. A year of double doors, let the doors swing wide open for us. I keep hearing to break out and break into. Break out of the old and break into a larger place, into the increase of God. I want all of my destiny and all God has for me. We are either being conformed into the world around us or being transformed by the renewing of our minds. Transformation will begin to redesign us towards the image of Christ. We must submit to the process to get where we need to be. There have been fragments all through our life and God is bringing those together to bring us towards our destiny.

First, realignment or being repositioned. Second, to be refined or have impurities and hidden faults and sins removed, and then finally we begin to be redesigned. God is not in the fast-food business. It takes time and our being willing to take up our cross and follow him. To open the door and let Him come in and spread that table before us, to reveal Himself to us that we might be revealed. A new image, a new design. If I want to be that good and faithful servant, if I want to see the power of God revealed through my life to others, I must go through the process.

Philippians 3:10 (AMPC) *"[For my determined purpose is] that I may know Him [that I may progressively become more deeply and intimately acquainted with Him, perceiving and recognizing and understanding the wonders of His person more strongly and more clearly], and that I may in that same way come to know the power outflowing from His resurrection [which it exerts over believers], and that I may so share His suffering as to be continually transformed [in spirit into His likeness even] to His death, [in the hope]."*

If we want His resurrection power in our lives and to have His glory rest on us, we have to learn also to partake in His suffering. How do we do that? We submit to the process of being redesigned. To take up our cross and follow Him. John 3:30 (AMPC) "He must increase, but I must decrease [He must grow more prominent, I must grow less so.] What is the final image? We begin to look more like Jesus. We begin to act more like Jesus and have His character, which is the fruit of the spirit spoken of in Galatians 5.

Luke 19:10 (NASB) *"For the Son of Man came to seek and save that which was lost."*

Yes, He came to save or make whole the lost, but it means much more than that. There were many things lost when Adam sinned. Adam was the first man and Jesus became the second man that He might make whole that which was lost by Adam. We are triune beings: body, soul, and spirit. Adam was not that way. He did not know that he had a body until he sinned. He did not know that he was even naked. He was spirit, soul, and body. The opposite of us. He was spirit ruled. His body was hidden we could say, it was on the inside of him. God had fellowship with him continually and gave him dominion over the earth in a beautiful world. It was like heaven on earth. He lost a lot. Jesus came to pay the price to restore man back to all that Adam lost. We can have that.

"Thy will be done on earth as it is in heaven is the father's prayer." We can be spirit ruled again. Our flesh war against our spirit.

Romans 12:1 (AMPC) *"Appeal to you therefore, brethren, and beg of you in view of [all] the mercies of God, to make a decisive dedication of your bodies [presenting all your members and faculties] as a living sacrifice, holy (devoted, consecrated) and well-pleasing to God, which is your reasonable (rational, intelligent) service and spiritual worship."*

Powerful! We do this by presenting all the members of our bodies as a living sacrifice. A decisive dedication!

That is the only way, submission with a decisive dedication. DDD. Decision Decides Destiny. Presenting all our faculties.

Faculties: a power or ability of the mind, our reasoning.

This is where the traditional church has gone wrong so many times and will be corrected by the process of Christ's Correction through the Holy Spirit to build His church. We have, by our reasoning, found forms of godliness that seemed good and we have missed God's best. We have had a form of Godliness and denied the power of God.

2 Timothy 3:5 (NASB) *"...holding to a form of godliness, although they have denied its power; Avoid such men as these."*

There have been programs, formulas, structures, and forms that the Holy Spirit, by God's grace, has even moved in. He is slowly removing His glory from those and beginning to build His Church where we will see His five-fold ascension gifts equip the saints to do the work of the ministry and begin to see the body build up the body as it wins the lost.

There are thousands of church members leaving the traditional church each year. They are tired of a form of godliness without any power. They are bored with the old way. They want more and they are not getting it. Many of these have been hurt and scared by the church.

I know that from personal experience of those close to me.

We now have over a million members of the body of Christ that have moved into house churches just in the U.S. Why? Because there they can have a Connection and be joined to a place where they can have true fellowship and see the lifeblood of Christ revealed. They begin to be part of the whole loaf. It almost seems like a pattern that was first laid down by the New Testament Church.

Does that mean that we can not meet in a building?

No, it does not. We just need to have the structure corrected and the Connection between the fivefold and their function and the members finding where they fit and what their function is.

This is one of the biggest places that the Church has missed badly. We are all ministers or servants in one way or the other. The season of the one-man show and shepherds feeding on the sheep is coming to an end.

Ez. 34:1-31 (AMPC) *"And the word of the Lord came to me, saying, Son of man, prophesy against the shepherds of Israel; prophesy and say to them, even to the [spiritual] shepherds of Israel who feed themselves! Should not the shepherds feed the sheep? You eat the fat, you clothe yourselves with the wool, you kill the fatling, but you do not feed the sheep. The diseased and weak you have not strengthened, the sick you have not healed, the hurt and crippled you have not bandage, those gone astray you have not brought back, the lost you have not sought to find, but with force and hardhearted harshness you have ruled them. And they were scattered because there was no shepherd, and when they were scattered, they became food for all the wild beasts of the field. My sheep wandered*

*through all the mountains and upon every high hill;
yes, My sheep were scattered upon all the face of
the earth and no one searched or sought for them.
Therefore, you [spiritual] shepherds, hear the word
of the Lord: As I live, says the Lord God, surely
because My sheep became a prey, and My sheep
became food for every beast of the field because
there was no shepherd, neither did my shepherds
search for My sheep, but the shepherds fed
themselves and fed not my sheep. Therefore, O you
[spiritual] shepherds, hear the word of the Lord:
Thus says the Lord God: Behold, I am against the
shepherds, and I will require My sheep at their hand
and cause them to cease feeding the sheep, neither
shall the shepherds feed themselves any more. I
will rescue My sheep from their mouths, that they
may not be food for them. For thus says the Lord
God: Behold, I Myself, will search for My sheep and
will seek them out. As a shepherd seeks out his
sheep in the day that he is among his flock that are
scattered, so will I seek out My sheep; and I will
rescue them out of all places where they have been
scattered in the day of cloud and thick darkness.
And I will bring them out from the peoples and*

gather them from the countries and will bring them to their own land; and I will feed them upon the mountains of Israel, by the watercourses, and in all the inhabited places of the country. I will feed them with good pasture, and upon the high mountains of Israel shall their fold be; there shall they lie down in a good fold, and in a fat pasture shall they feed upon the mountains of Israel. I will feed My sheep and I will cause them to lie down, say the Lord God. I will seek that which was lost and bring back that which has strayed, and I will bandage the hurt and the crippled and will strengthen the weak and the sick, but I will destroy the fat and the strong [who have become hardhearted and perverse]; I will feed them with judgment and punishment." And as for you, O My flock, thus says the Lord God; Behold, I judge between sheep and sheep, between the rams and the great he-goats [the malicious and the tyrants of the pasture]. Is it too little for you that you feed on the best pasture? And to have drunk of the waters clarified by subsiding, but you must foul the rest of the water with your feet? And My flock, must they feed on what your feet have trodden and drink what your feet have fouled? Therefore thus says the

Lord God to them: Behold, I Myself, will judge between fat sheep and impoverished sheep, or fat goats and lean goats. Because you push with side and with shoulder and thrust with your horns all those that have become weak and diseased, till you have scattered them abroad. Therefore will I rescue My flock, and they shall no more be a prey; and I will judge between sheep and sheep. And I will raise up over them one Shepherd and He shall feed them, even My Servant David; He shall feed them and He shall be their Shepherd. And I the Lord will be their God and My Servant David will be a Prince among them; I the Lord have spoken. I will confirm with them a covenant of peace and will cause the evil beasts to cease out of the land, and [My people] shall dwell safely in the wilderness, desert, or pastureland and sleep [confidently] in the woods. And I will make them and places round about My hill a blessing, and I will cause the showers to come down in their season; there shall be showers of blessing [of good insured by God's favor]. And the tree of the field shall yield its fruit and the earth shall yield its increase; and [My people] shall be secure in their land, and they shall be confident and know (understand and realize) that I am the Lord, when I have broken the bars of their yoke and have delivered them out of the hand of those who made slaves of them. And they shall no more be a prey to the nations, nor shall the beasts of the earth devour them, but they shall dwell safely and none shall make them afraid [in the day of the Messiah' reign]. And I will raise up for them a planting of crops for renown, and they shall be no more consumed with hunger in the land nor bear the reproach of the nations any longer. Then shall they know [positively] that I, the Lord their God, am with them and that they, the house of Israel, are My people, says the Lord God. And that you, My sheep the sheep of My pasture, are [only] men and I am your God, says the Lord God."

No, not all Shepherds feed on the sheep. God is raising up Shepherds after His heart that feed the sheep. Too many move out of reasoning and un-renewed minds and have built up their own kingdoms and wrong structures that do not equip the saints or fit them into their proper function, role or service.

There is a way out. We must repent and submit to the Correction, God's first step in His process for the Church. It is happening and will flow into His second step of Connection or the joining of His body together to see it build itself up.

Submitting to Correction for judgment comes first to the House of God. He will design us. He loves us so much that He still corrects us and makes whole that which was lost. We will be made into the image of God.

CHAPTER THREE

CONNECTION

The second step of His process is Connection. This brings construction or a building up of the Body of Christ after the Correction has taken place.

This can overlap with Correction and can flow together. He begins to build His Church fitting each member into his proper place and function or role. We then begin to see a glorious Body of Christ being formed. We will begin to see the full statue or the full man of Christ coming forth. His bride without spot or blemish being made into the full stature of Christ. Correction will bring Connection.

If I want to find my destiny, I must find my proper place and function and see what I was formed to be. I have to especially do this until He brings the final step of Completion, maturity, or the full stature of Christ. We must see to be!

Where is your proper place and function? Where do you fit and connect? Who will help you find your place and function that you may become all that God wants you to be? You must find it! If you are where you are not finding your proper place, function, and have no Connection, then you need to move. Do not die on the vine just cause you like the people there. God never expects His sheep to stay in a pasture where they are not getting fed and being put into their proper function.

Looking at Ephesians 4:16 we see some of what Connection looks like.

Ephesians 4:16 (AMPC) *"For because of Him the whole body (the church, in all its various parts), closely joined and firmly knit together by the joint and ligaments with which it is supplied, when each part [with power adapted to its need] is working properly [in all its functions], grows to full maturity, building itself up in love."*

It says we are joined together, or could we say, connected together and firmly knit together by the joints that supplies. Joints are relationships. We have to have relationships to be able to be supplied to and find where we fit and what our function or role is. Once this happens then we are in a place to grow into maturity or Completion.

The New Testament Church experienced this. They learned what fellowship was all about. They knew each other very well.

Acts 2:44 (AMPC) *"And all who believed (who adhered to and trusted in and relied on Jesus Christ) were united and [together] they had everything in common;"*

The word fellowship (koinonia) actually means to have a common life. Koinonia is the anglicization of Greek word (koivovia) actually means communion by intimate participation.

When we get into relationships and are connected to such a degree that life flows from one to another, only then will we see the Body of Christ being built up as it should be. The flow of life happens in the natural as well as the spiritual. The natural comes before the supernatural.

Where do I fit?

Where am I connected?

God sets us by the Holy Spirit into the local body as He pleases. If we are not under Apostolic oversight, where new foundations and Corrections can begin, then we will have a hard time finding our proper place, function, or role.

The Holy Spirit will reveal to us our place of service. We then have to submit to it under the proper leadership and one of the fivefold ascension anointings of the Church that Christ gave to us for the equipping of the saints to do the work of the ministry.

Do you get the picture? It is not a one-man show, but a plurality of leadership, working together so each member can find where he fits and what his function or role is so the body can build up the body.

Our religious traditions have cheated us out of God's best by keeping us locked into these structures that once seemed good!

I do not want just good—I want God's best. The status quo must go.

By God's grace, He is still working in traditional churches. He still anoints there, it is just restricted. Tradition makes the word God wants to give for Correction of no effect. Tradition says the old is good enough.

He is making us become what we need to be.

Hebrews 13:21 (AMPC) "Strengthen (complete, perfect) and make you what you ought to be and equip you with everything good that you may carry out His will; [while He Himself] works in you and accomplishes that which is pleasing in His sight, through Jesus Christ (the Messiah); to Whom be the glory forever and ever (to the ages of the ages). *Amen (so be it)"*

We do not want religious traditions that make His word of no effect.

You will come under one or more of the five-fold ascension anointings of the Church. In the past, we have been pastor-dominated, with the pastor doing all the work and very few members ever being equipped. We just found ourselves sitting in pews listening to nice sermons. I don't need any more nice sermons. I need to be in the right place functioning as God intended.

We were part of a 'bless me club', as a lot of churches have become: good entertainment centers, affecting the emotions of people. The church cannot move out of their emotions. Just good feelings are not what will get us where we need to go.

I need someone to teach me and train me how to be equipped to do the work of the ministry. Will someone please activate me into my proper place and function? Thank God I have found that place. I am in the right place at the right time.

Not all are Prophets, but all can prophesy. There needs to be all five ascension offices, graces, or anointings in place in each Church.

Ephesians 2:20 (AMPC) *"You are built upon the foundation of the Apostles and Prophets with Christ Jesus Himself the chief Cornerstone."*

The cornerstone is the part of the building that aligns the rest of the building to be straight and in proper order. Apostles and Prophets begin to bring order and set foundations that we can build on.

With the foundation in order, our Connection and proper relationship with each other starts to flow out of our relationship with Christ!

Building upon the five-fold foundation, our church leadership can help establish fellowship in the church, using the five-fold gifts that God gave us. We will only go as far or as high as our leadership goes. We must pray for all leaders in the body of Christ that this foundation will be corrected. The Body of Christ will build itself up when it gets in proper Connection, when the lifeblood of Christ, or fellowship, beings to flow between believers.

It is coming and has begun to trickle into many over the centuries. We have just not seen it on the whole. We are beginning to see a shift into the right order and a Correction begin to take place. The real Church soon will not look the same or function the same way. We have let too much of the world's system and mold affect the Church and have not let the Kingdom of God rule as it should.

The five-fold offices or graces are part of God's government.

Isaiah 9:6-7 (AMPC) *"For to us a Child is born, to us a Son is given; and the government shall be upon His shoulder, and His name shall be called Wonderful, Counselor, Mighty God, Everlasting Father [of Eternity], Prince of Peace. Of the increase of His government and of peace there shall be no end, upon the throne of David and over His kingdom, to establish it and to uphold it with justice and with righteousness from the [latter] time forth, even forevermore. The zeal of the Lord of host will perform this. From the later time forth."*

God by the Holy Spirit is always increasing. His kingdom and government are effected through His five-fold ascension anointings of the Church.

Hebrews 13:17 (AMPC) *"Obey your spiritual leaders and submit to them [continually recognizing their authority over you], for they are constantly keeping watch over your souls and guarding your spiritual welfare, as men who will have to render and account [of their trust]. [Do your part to] let them do this with gladness and not with sighing and groaning, for that would not be profitable to you [either]."*

Let us begin to understand we are in the government of God. We are in the Kingdom of God, and we serve a King and those He has set in place of five-fold leadership. We are either being conformed into something or being transformed into His kingdom.

Let us begin to move into the proper Connection that it will bring the full results of His kingdom. We were made to rule.

Revelation 5:10 (AMPC) *"And you have made them a kingdom (royal race) and priests to God, and they shall reign [as kings] over the earth."*

The first commission that God gave Adam was to rule and take dominion. He desires to restore all that Adam lost when he sinned. That is our example. Let's get connected and see the full stature of Christ begin to be formed in us, with the lifeblood of Christ our fellowship beginning to flow.

CHAPTER FOUR

COMPLETION

Completion is the fulfillment of the process after Correction and Connection have taken place. Completion means maturity, the individual believer being fully grown. It can also mean to be made perfect or complete.

Christ is coming back for a full-grown Church, a bride that is without spot or blemish.

2 Peter (AMPC) 3:14 *"So beloved , since you are expecting these things, for eager to be found by Him [at His coming] without spot or blemish and at peace [in serene confidence, free from fears and agitating passions and moral conflicts]."*

Christ will build His Church and the gates of hell will not prevail against it.

There is no growth without change. There is no direction without Correction. We have to be willing to leave the old behind and find new patterns for our lives. We must begin to change patterns individually and corporately. We cannot keep doing the same thing that has been laid down by our forefathers.

We must have a paradigm shift. Greek= paradeigma = pattern. A shift of patterns. I know when I want things to change in my life it means some patterns will change, and I will grow. I want to grow into that mature man and be more like Christ.

That is exactly what will happen as the Body of Christ goes through the process of Correction to Connection to finally Completion. Let us become all that God wants to make us become.

Submission to the process is the key. That means laying down our own will and rights and moving out of the old into the new. The Holy Spirit is beginning to peel off the layer of the old wineskin and beginning to reveal the new wineskin.

He has a destiny for us and it can be found in the processes of God.

Sacrifice, Servant, Soldier, And Son

There are four positions we must take in the process. The four positions are the position of a sacrifice, a servant, a soldier, and a son.

Sacrifice is the first position we need to take. Sacrifice has to be coupled with obedience.

Romans (AMPC) 12:1 *"I appeal to you therefore, brethren, and beg of you in view of [all] the mercies of God, to make a decisive dedication of your bodies [presenting all your members and faculties] as a living sacrifice, holy (devoted, consecrated) and well pleasing to God, which is your reasonable (rational, intelligent) service and spiritual worship."*

We see through the Bible that God always requires us to sacrifice that which He has given us. He gave the ultimate sacrifice in His Son and resurrected Him to a place beside Him and gave eternal life through the sacrifice. As with Abraham, He required the promise and destiny that He had been given to be sacrificed. Abraham realized even if God required his son as a sacrifice, that God would resurrect him again. We see that God provided a sacrifice to take the place of Abraham's son after He saw Abraham's obedience.

God wants the same thing from us. Whatever He gives us, He wants back. He wants it in His hands and not ours. He resurrects it and brings life to it. If we will take the position of our lives being a sacrifice, and give it back to Him, we will see resurrection life in our lives and in our ministry. We must realize that without God doing it, it will be another form of religion that operates out of our own performance. We need to become instruments in God's hands letting Him use us as He wills. His ways becoming our ways.

Matt. 6:10 (NASB) *"Your kingdom come, Your will be done on earth as it is in heaven."*

Matt 6:33(AMPC) *"But seek first (aim and strive after) first of all His kingdom and His righteousness (His way of doing and being right), and then all these things (taken together will be given you besides."*

Religion has been trying to get earth to heaven, and we must be about getting heaven to earth. His will be done on earth as it is in heaven. God moved with His power after a sacrifice was given. He only accepted the sacrifice when it was given in obedience from the heart. Let us look at one of those times when God moved with His mighty power after a sacrifice.

2 Kings 3:9-24 (AMPC) *So the king of Israel went with the king of Judah and the king of Edom. They made a circuit of seven days journey, but there was no water for the army or for the animals following them. Then the king of Israel said, Alas! The Lord has called [us] three kings together to be delivered into Moab's hand! But Jehoshaphat said, Is there no prophet of the Lord here by whom we may inquire of the Lord? One of the kings of Israel's servants answered, Elisha son of Shaphat, who served Elijah, is here. Jehoshaphat said, The word of the Lord is with him. So Joram king of Israel and Jehoshaphat and the king of Edom went down to Elisha. And Elisha said to the king of Israel. What have I to do with you? Go to the prophets of your*

[wicked] father Ahab and your [wicked] mother Jezebel. But the king of Israel said to him. No, for the Lord has called [us] three kings together to be delivered into the hand of Moab. And Elisha said, As the Lord of hosts lives, before Whom I stand, surely, were it not that I respect the presence of Jehoshaphat king of Judah, I would neither look at you nor see you [King Joram]. But now bring me a minstrel. And while the minstrel played, the hand and power of the Lord came upon [Elisha]. And he said, Thus says the Lord: Make this [dry] brook bed full of trenches. For thus says the Lord: You shall not see wind or rain, yet that ravine shall be filled with water, so you, your cattle, and your beasts [of burden] may drink. This is but a light thing in the sight of the Lord, He will deliver the Moabites also into your hand. You shall smite every fenced city and every fenced city and every choice city, and shall fell every good tree and stop all wells of water and mark every good piece of land with stones. In the morning, when the sacrifice was offered, behold, there came water by the way of Edom, and the country was filled with water. When all the Moabites heard that the kings had come up to fight

against them, all who were able to put on armor, young and old, gathered and drew up at the border. When they rose up early next morning, and the sun shone upon the water, the Moabites saw the water across from them as red as blood. And they said, This is blood; the kings have surely been fighting and have slain one another. Now then, Moab, to the spoil! But when they came to the camp of Israel, the Israelites rose up and smote the Moabites, so that they fled before them. And they went forward, slaying the Moabites as they went.

So we see the Prophet in verse nine say the water you want will not come by normal means. There will be no wind or rain as normal. It only happens after the next morning when they had offered a sacrifice to the Lord. It was then that the breakthrough came and water flooded down from the mountain. Sometimes we need the water of the Holy Spirit to flood us so we can have a breakthrough. Not only that, but God uses this miracle to defeat their enemy. We see this over and over, as God required then provided through a sacrifice.

Malachi 3 says if we will give to God our provision then He will open the windows of heaven, pour out a blessing and rebuke the devourer of our enemy for us. If you want a breakthrough then sow with a sacrifice or offering and see what God might do for you.

I can hear some saying, "That's the Old Testament and not for today." But the Old Testament is full of types and shadows for us to apply to our lives today.

Joel 2:14 (AMPC) *"Who knows but what He will turn, revoke your sentence [of evil], and leave a blessing behind Him [of evil], and leave a blessing behind Him [giving you the means with which to serve him], even a cereal or meal offering and a drink offering for the Lord, your God?"*

We see here what I call the cycle of giving. He will leave a blessing behind that you might serve Him and give back to Him. He gave to you, so you can give to Him, so He can give back to you. God desires that you show Him trust and relationship as the only provider by offering yourself and all that you have as a sacrifice so He can move on your behalf.

Let's look at some other scriptures that speak about our sacrifice.

Philippians 4:18 (NASB) *"But I have received everything in full and have and abundance; I am amply supplied, having received from Epaphroditus what you have sent, a fragrant aroma, an acceptable sacrifice, well-pleasing to God."*

Ephesians 5:1 (NASB) *"Therefore be imitators of God, as beloved children; And walk in love, just as Christ also loved you and gave Himself up for us, an offering and a sacrifice to God as a fragrant aroma."*

Romans 12:1 (NASB) *"Therefore I urge you, brothers and sisters, by the mercies of God, to present your bodies as a living and holy sacrifice, acceptable to God, which is your spiritual service of worship."*

*

The second position we must take is as a servant.

The Church likes to say minister, but that word is not used in most translations. It is best to use the word servant or slave. We are all servants of God first and then used by Him to be servants to others, especially to the household of God.

1 John 3:16 (AMPC) *"By this we come to know (progressively to recognize, to perceive, to understand) the [essential] love: that He laid down His [own] life for us; and we ought to lay [our] lives down for [those who are our] brothers [in Him]."*

The process is progressive. No one is above being a servant and having the attitude or position of a servant. The last thing that we always will want to hear is "enter in my good and faithful servant" not that you preached some good sermons to some people in the pews.

Matthew 20:26-27 (NASB) *"It is not this way among you, but whoever wishes to become great among you shall be your servant, and whoever wishes to be first among you shall be your slave."*

Matthew 23:10-11 (NASB) *"Do not be called leaders; for One is your Leader, that is, Christ, but the greatest among you shall be your servant."*

Romans 1:1 (NASB) *"Paul, a bond-servant of Christ Jesus, called as an apostle, set apart for the gospel of God,"*

Paul considered himself a bond-servant. In Bible days, a servant (slave) was to be released in the year of jubilee. If he chose, he could stay with his master. If he chose, he would remain a slave or servant to his master and be a bond-servant the rest of his life. The master would make him his forever by bringing him to the doorpost and marking his ear as his own.

WOW! May we be marked for Christ as His bond-servant. We have an example by Christ who said, "I did not come to be served but, to be a servant to all."

Philippians 2:5-7 (AMPC) *"Let this same attitude and purpose and [humble] mind be in you which was in Christ Jesus: [Let Him be your example in humility]. Who, although being essentially one with*

God and in the form of God [possessing the fullness of the attributes which make God God], did not think this equality with God was a thing to be eagerly grasped or retained, but stripped Himself [of all privileges and rightful dignity], so as to assume the guise of a servant (slave), in that He became like men and was born a human being."

Mark 10:45 (NASB) *"For even the Son of Man did not come to be served, but to serve, and to give His life a ransom for many."*

All the Prophets and men of God in the Bible were considered God's servants. We are instruments in God's hand and His servant. We see Jesus and men of God lived this out by serving others. There is a great book on serving by Charles Swindol called *Improving Your Serve.*

May we all learn to take the position of a servant.

God resists the proud but gives grace to the humble. It is time that those in leadership learn these lessons. The word leadership is mentioned less than a dozen times in the Bible but the word servant is mentioned 900 times. All the great men of God I have ever seen or known had one quality in common, and that was they had a humble spirit.

When you are a slave or servant everything is furnished for you. Christ has furnished the complete work to equip us to be a good and faithful servant (slave). A good servant has determination and dedication. He fulfills several things.

(1) Obeys orders.

(2) Fulfills the desires of his master.

(3) Pleases his master.

(4) Performs his duties

(5) Has no rights of His own.

All us like sheep have gone astray because we have gone our own way.

We also see that if we are a good servant it means that we will be a good steward of what we've been given. Stewardship means the management of resources that belong to someone else. God is our source and everything that we have is from Him and belongs to Him.

Matthew 25:14-29 (AMPC) *"For it is like a man who was about to take a long journey, and he called his servants together and entrusted them with his property. To one he gave five talents [probably about $5000], to another two, to another one- to each in proportion to his own personal ability. Then he departed and left the country. He who had received the five talents went at once and traded with them, and he gained five talents more. And likewise who had received the two talents he also gained two talents more. But he who had received the one talent went and dug a hole in the ground and hid his master's money. Now after a long time the master of those servants returned and settled accounts with them. And he who had received the five talents came and brought him five more, saying, Master, you entrusted to me five talents; see, here I have gained five talents more. His master said to him, Well done, you upright (honorable admirable) and faithful and trustworthy over a little; I will put you in charge of much. Enter into and share the joy (delight, the blessedness) which your master enjoys. And he also who had the two talents came forward, saying, Master, you entrusted two talents* to me; here I have gained two talents more. His master said to him, Well done, you upright (honorable, admirable) and faithful servant! You have been faithful and trustworthy over a little; I will put you in charge of much. Enter into and share the joy (the delight, the blessedness) which your master enjoys. He who had received one talent also came forward, saying, Master, I knew you to a harsh and hard man, reaping where you did not sow, and gathering where you had not winnowed [the gain]. So I was afraid. and I went and hid your talent in the ground. Here you have what is your own. But his master answered him, You wicked and lazy and idle servant! Did you indeed know that I reap where I have not sowed and gather [grain] where I have not winnowed? Then you should have invested my money with the bankers, and at my coming I would have received what was my own with interest. So take the talent away from him and give it to the one who has the ten talents. For to everyone who has more will be given, and he will be furnished richly so that he will have an abundance; but from the one who does not have, even what he does have will be taken away. "

The Lord wants to bless us, if we will get in the right position with the right attitude. We must learn not to hold on to our rights and that which God has given us. If we will put it back in His hand and use that which He has given us by instruction through the Holy Spirit we will begin to see a degree of multiplication in everything we do. We must give ourselves away to God who wants to give Himself to us.

*

The third position we must take is that of a soldier.

2 Timothy 2:3-4 (AMPC) *"Take [with me] your share of the hardships and suffering [which you are called to endure] as a good (first-class) soldier of Christ Jesus. No soldier when in service gets entangled in the enterprises of [civilian life]; his aim is to satisfy and please the one who enlisted him."*

Philippians 2:25 (AMPC) *"However, I thought it necessary to send Epaphroditus [back] to you. [He has been] my brother and companion in labor and my fellow soldier, as well as [having come as] your special messenger (apostle) and minister to my need."*

1 Corinthians 9:7 (AMPC) *"Consider this: What soldier at any time serves at his own expense."*

Ephesians 6:10-18 (AMPC) *"In conclusion, be strong in the Lord [be empowered through your union with Him that strength which His boundless might provides]. Put on God's whole armor [the armor of a heavy–armed soldier which God supplies], that you may be able successfully to stand up against [all] the strategies and the deceits of the devil. For we are not wrestling with flesh and blood [contending only with physical opponents], but against the despotisms, against the powers, against [the master spirits who are] the world rulers of this present darkness, against the spirit forces of wickedness in the heavenly (supernatural) sphere. Therefore put on God's complete armor, that you may be able to resist and stand your ground on the evil day [of danger], and, having done all [the crisis demands], to stand [firmly in your place]. Stand therefore [hold your ground], having tightened the belt of truth around your loins and having put on the breastplate of integrity and of moral rectitude and right standing with God, And having shod your fee in preparation [to face the enemy with the firm-footed stability, the promptness, and the readiness produced by the good news] of the Gospel of peace. Lift up over all the [covering] shield of saving faith, upon which you can quench all the flaming missiles of the wicked [one]. And take the helmet of salvation and the sword that the Spirit wield, which is the Word of God. Pray at all times (on every occasion, in every season) in the Spirit, with all [manner of] prayer and entreaty. To what end keep alert and watch with strong purpose and perseverance, interceding on behalf of all the saints (God's consecrated people)." We see we should learn what it means to be a good and faithful soldier. We need to find our place in the army of God. Some might be on the front line as a fivefold minister (servant) and some might be behind the lines supporting as intercessors or in other places of service. We all have a rank and a file that we fit in.*

Joel 2:7-8 (NASB) "They run like mighty men; they climb the wall like men of war, and they do not break their ranks. Neither does one thrust upon another; they walk everyone in his path, And they burst through and upon the weapons, yet they are not wounded and do not change their course."

We are in a war of life and death. We must fight.

2 Corinthians 10:4 (AMPC) *"For the weapons of our warfare are not physical [weapons of flesh and blood], but they are mighty before God for the overthrow and destruction of strongholds,"*

Ephesians 6:12 (AMPC) *"For we are not wrestling with flesh and blood [contending only with physical opponents], but against the despotisms, against [the master spirits who are] the world rulers of this present darkness, against the spirit forces of wickedness in the heavenly (supernatural) sphere."*

We are constantly in a war for ourselves, our family, and our brothers and sisters. We need to learn what our weapons are. We need to learn how to use the word of God as our sword along with prayer. We must learn how to use the gifts of the spirit in spiritual warfare such as the word of wisdom and knowledge along with the discerning of spirits. We need to know first what we are fighting against and get the proper strategy from the Holy Spirit and become victorious. We must learn to walk in unity. There is power in agreement.

Matthew 18:19 (NASB) *"Again I say unto you, That if two of you shall agree on earth as touching any thing that they shall ask, it shall be done for them of my Father which is in heaven."*

*

I have learned there is even a higher place than being a sacrifice, servant or a soldier. That is to be a son or daughter of God the Father.

Romans 8:14 (AMPC*) "For all who are led by the Spirit of God are sons of God."* Romans 8:19 (NASB) *"For the anxious longing of the creation waits eagerly for the revealing of the sons of God."* Ephesians 1:5 (NASB) *"He predestined us to adoption as sons through Jesus Christ to Himself, according to the kind intention of His will."*

Our Father has always wanted a family from the beginning. That was his original intent. To be able to have that koinonia, a sharing of a common life,

with His family. That is still His purpose. We all
have many brothers and sisters in the family of
God. Past, present, and future.

Awaken

Awaken, o people of God, for God by His Holy
Spirit is ringing the alarm bell to His people. He is
calling for the gifts and callings that have laid
asleep and been dormant to begin to arise and
come forth.

Join the army of God. He is calling his people into
a new place. We first must learn how to leave the
old and be corrected into the original design that
He has for us. We must get connected in the right
place and begin to function in our proper roles.

We then can see God bringing us to the final
Completion and full stature of Christ. Submit to
the process and take your rightful position and
begin to see God do miracles, signs, and wonders
in your life.

What a time to be alive!

Let us not do what religion has done in the past and just settle for what seems to be good, but let us look for God's best. This is our time to move into the destiny God has for us. God does not make mistakes. We are here at this time for a certain destiny. According to Jeremiah 1:5, that destiny was determined by God before we were ever born.

Find your place and function. Find your destiny. Pull your future into your present.

Remember: Decision, Decides, Destiny, and Desperation and persistence will be the path.

CHAPTER FIVE

FINDING OUR DESTINY

Every destiny is always wrapped up in the will of God. If we find out the will of God for our lives every day, we will soon find out where our destiny resides.

So how do I find the will of God for my life? I must first learn what the word of God says, whether through the logos word or a rhema word. Logos is defined as the word of God that has already been spoken and recorded in the Bible. Rhema is defined as the word of God that is being spoken now or a present tense word, a new fresh word.

We can hear God out of the Bible when he makes it a rhema word to us. He can also speak directly to you at any time through any means He desires. I find the best time to hear from the Holy Spirit is when I am quiet inside myself.

Psalms 37:7 (AMPC) *"Be still and rest in the Lord; wait for Him and patiently lean yourself upon Him, fret not yourself because of him who prospers in his way, because of the man that brings wicked devices to pass.*"

The word "still" means to chill out, drop your hand, and stop from your work. The word "rest" means to be quiet inside ourselves. Only through spending time being quiet and listening will you be able to hear more clearly. I find one of my best times to hear is after I have spent time worshiping and fellowshipping with the Lord in prayer.

Prayer should always be a place of conversation. This means at times you are talking to God and other times He is talking to you. The key is to reach that silent place of rest.

Some of my best times of prayer are when I do not say a word.

The longer we practice this the easier it will be to get to a quiet place in ourselves and begin to hear more clearly. This gets us back again to Romans 12, concerning the command to present to God our bodies, attitudes, and abilities, which are our positions and faculties.

The thing we have to fear is that God will let us have our own way. This brings us back to that keyword "submission". As your mind is renewed, you begin to receive new positions you are to take. It is a great place to be, and we need it every single day. Most of the time this process has to start with repentance.

Repentance is a progressive process, of changing old patterns of life into new ones. We have been taught so much about His promises but not His process. We must submit to the process and let the Holy Spirit train us in all truth.

We see in James 4:8 (NASB) *"Draw near to God and He will draw near to you. Cleanse your hands you sinners; and purify your hearts, you double-minded."*

Here we find revelation of two relationships, one toward God, and one toward our fellow man. That is what our cross is all about: a vertical relationship to God, and a horizontal relationship to our fellow man.

What is our cross?

Our cross is when our will crosses with His. Step one is to draw near to God. You do this simply by coming toward God. Normally in prayer, but prayer can be anywhere at any time. The second step is to cleanse our hands. This speaks of our relationship with others and how we have dealt with others. This can be outward or inward in our attitudes. Third, it says to purify our hearts. This concerns the position with which we come to God and our relationship to Him.

As we position ourselves to receive, we will begin to hear more and more clearly. We have spiritual ears and eyes. We see this in Isaiah 6:10 (NASB) *"Render the hearts of this people insensitive. Their ears dull, And their eyes dim, Otherwise they might see with their eyes, Hear with their ear, Understand with their hearts, And return and be healed."*

There are many great points in that verse. Most of us are insensitive in positioning ourselves to listen to God. When we begin to understand this and repent, we are on the path to the place of hearing. We can pray for the Holy Spirit to help clean our ears and eyes of that which makes them dull of hearing and dim to see. For what we see, we can be.

When we daily spend time in fellowship with the Lord, the Holy Spirit renews our mind. We go through the process of positioning ourselves to receive and be in the right position before God. Being right before God, actually means to be righteous, not religious. That is what God is looking for. If we are right before God, then we must be right with our fellow man.

The Holy Spirit often uses the language of dreams and visions, which means images, to speak to us. He can also speak directly to us in our thoughts or our spirit. A dream or a vision will take interpretation. If you cannot receive an interpretation for yourself then you can go to someone with spiritual authority that sees for themselves. A vision can be an open vision when you see things in front of you, and it can also be in your mind or spirit. There is a great teaching by John Paul Jackson on dreams and visions and their interpretation.

The key to hearing and seeing is submission to the process. Position yourself to hear and see. Let us ask the Holy Spirit to help us. We have not because we ask not. In our processes with God, we will find ourselves many times in repentance as he shows us areas that need to be corrected. This Correction means a place where we are changing our position and changing our minds.

With repentance, we can keep our relationship and communication with God open and clear. Some in religious circles think you only have to repent once. God forbid this attitude.

If we are not repenting in our lives continually, then our minds are not being renewed. For when we position ourselves right and spend time with God, we will have our minds renewed and see ourselves repenting of the old way.

The Lord has a new day that is ahead with an ongoing process for us to be able to reach into higher spiritual levels. We see in Revelation, the seven churches had one thing in common.

Rev. 2:7 (NASB) *"He who has an ear, let him hear what the Spirit says to the churches."*

Each church had problems that the Apostle John was addressing for Correction. Each had the common problem of hearing and seeing what position they were to take. We have the same problem today as tradition keeps churches from hearing.

Why?

Mark 7:13 (AMP) *"so you nullify the [authority of the] word of God [acting as if it did not apply] because of your tradition which you have handed down [through the elders]. And you do many things such as this."* Another translation says you make the word of God of no effect for the sake of your tradition.

Tradition says we know what God wants to do and how he wants to do it. We have the same problem that Adam and Eve had. The devil said "Hasn't God said:" It seemed good. It looked good. By their own reason, they said it was good.

The amazing thing is by God's grace, at times, He still will work in that circle. What happens is we settle for what we think looks good, out of our own reasoning, and totally miss God's best. We have smiley sermons preached to smiley people in pews and no one hardly changes, grows, or is activated into their proper function. I could not survive in most churches.

There are thousands of people leaving the church every year. I have recently talked to Christian folks that have left the church. They told me one of two things. One, that they have been deeply hurt and have scars from the church; and two, they saw needy people looked down on and not helped. I heard a story of a man who said he was in our country for ten years and no one shared Jesus with him until he went to another country.

What has the church become? Some are no more than glorified clubs and entertainment platforms to please people. Our duty as ministers was never to please people; it was to be servants of the most high God and his servant and to please Him.

If we take any other attitude other than that of a servant to God and those around us, then we are in sin and do not even know it. I pray God will open the eyes of ministers to that. We have put people in the wrong place and called them pastors, or whatever, and it was not meant to be.

We can learn some things by reading in Revelation what their lack of hearing and seeing produced. They were dull of hearing and dim of seeing what they should do and become. They were not able to perceive how they should be corrected.

Correction brings Connection and Connection brings Completion (maturity and the full stature of Christ). When we hear and we see what we need to hear and see, it positions us for the future and for our true destiny. It gives us a new image of who God is and who we are to become. We need to learn to hear and see and pull the future into our present and into our lives every day. We need to activate our future and our destiny. We do not live out of our reasoning, but out of a renewed mind and the mind of Christ. We are to live by the spirit, not the flesh.

When we begin to do this we will see God suddenly begin to respond to our faith. For faith comes by hearing.

Romans 10:17 (NASB) *"So faith comes from hearing, and hearing by the word of God."*

The kingdom of God runs on faith and hearing from God.

Matthew 4:4 (NASB) *But He answered and said, "It is written, man shall not live on bread alone, but every word that proceeds out of the mouth of God."*

The "word" in that verse means we are living by that which we hear every day. Christ said, "I do not do anything less I hear the Father say it." What do you think he did when He prayed all night? He was listening to the Father. We must eat bread naturally every day, and we must have the bread of life spiritually by receiving rhema (a word spoken for now) every day.

Religion and tradition taught us to let others hear for us. That was never God's intention. It is His intention that everyone can hear if they position themselves correctly.

Our destiny lies in our hearing and seeing. God often reveals things to us through oracular intimation. Those are big words for me and probably some of you. Oracular means giving forth utterances or decisions as if by special inspiration of authority. Intimation means a hint or suggestion. This happens frequently to people of God who walk by the Spirit of God. It happens through dreams, visions, trances, and even through imagination. These are never clear. We always see in part and only get part of the puzzle.

1 Corinthians 13:12 (AMPC) *"For now we are looking in a mirror that give only a dim (blurred) reflection [of reality as in a riddle or enigma], but then [when perfection comes] we shall see in reality and face to face! Now I know in part (imperfectly), but then I shall know and understand fully and clearly, even in the same manner as I have been fully and clearly, even in the same manner as I have been fully and clearly known and understood [by God]."*

The Holy Spirit will lead us to the end of the journey and many times through natural means. The supernatural is not always spectacular.

We need to always have our antennas up. Awareness and perception is the prerequisite of the prophetic or the Holy Spirit directing us. I call these times "glimpses" that the Holy Spirit gives us. They are normally short times of images that will come to us.

These prophetic glimpses normally follow a pattern of progressive understanding over time. First, there will be partial understanding. Second, there will be advanced or expanded understanding. Third, a promise of the future will be revealed within the vision.

The promise always speaks to our potential.

As written in a previous portion, we will need an interpretation of what we see. Sometimes we get this immediately, and other times we will need to seek out the interpretation. We need to be tuned in so we can recognize when He speaks.

There are three voices that we can hear: our own voice, the enemy's voice, and the Holy Spirit's voice. We need to walk in step with Spirit so we can truly determine His voice and the images that we receive.

Through practice and over time of receiving from the Holy Spirit, we will be clear in our hearing and imagination.

The Holy Spirit can also reveal our destiny to us through others, especially the Apostles and the Prophets that God has appointed for us. We will find ourselves moving into our functions and roles and what our destiny is as we submit to the processes of God.

CHAPTER SIX

THE THREE D's

1) DECISION: Decision means choice in what we yield or submit to. We have a choice of going our way or submitting to the will of God and pleasing Him. This is the place that we learn to die to ourselves and our own way. Our carnal nature fights and wars against the spirit.

Romans 8:7-8 (AMPC) *[That is] because the mind of the flesh or [with its carnal thoughts and purposes] is hostel to God, for it does no submit itself to God's Law; indeed it cannot, "So then those who are living the life of the flesh [catering to the appetites and impulses of their carnal nature] cannot please or satisfy God, or be acceptable to Him."*

Matthew 16:24 (AMPC) *Then Jesus said to His disciple, "If anyone desires to be My disciple, let him deny himself and take up his cross and follow Me [cleave steadfastly to Me, conform wholly to My example in living and, if need be, in dying, also]."*

I have found that my decision has to be mixed with my desire. Decision decides destiny.

2) DEDICATION: Only after you have made the decision can you then be in a position to dedicate yourself. Dedication always means having discipline. Being a disciple says we have dedication with discipline.

Romans 12:1 (AMPC) *"I appeal to you therefore, brethren, and beg of you in view of [all] the mercies of God, to make a decisive dedication of your bodies [presenting all your members and faculties] as a living sacrifice, holy (devoted, consecrated) and well pleasing to God, which is your reasonable (rational, intelligent) service and spiritual worship."*

Matthew 16:24 (AMPC) *"Then Jesus said to His disciples, If anyone desires to be My disciple, let him deny himself [disregard, lose sight of, and forget himself and his own interests] and take up his cross and follow Me [cleave steadfastly to Me, conform wholly to My example in living and, if need be, in dying, also]."*

What is our cross? It is where our will crosses with God's. That is the place we can deny ourselves and die to our will and our rights. Dedication always has devotion, devotion to the King and what pleases Him.

3) DISCIPLE: We need to learn what it means to be a true disciple. We see in the scripture above in Matthew 16:24 (AMPC), being a disciple means we must deny ourselves and our own way. We cannot be led by our own understanding, knowledge, and reasoning. We must seek the knowledge of God.

Proverbs 3:5 (AMPC) *"Lean on, trust in, and be confident in the Lord with all your heart and mind and do not rely on your own insight or understanding."*

Our knowledge will puff us up. His knowledge will humble us so we can be the disciple that He is looking for.

Ephesians 1:17 (version) *"[for I always pray to] the God of our Lord Jesus Christ, the Father of glory, that He may grant you a spirit of wisdom and revelation [of insight into mysteries and secrets] in this [deep and intimate] knowledge of Him."*

Three of the seven spirits of the Lord in Isaiah 11:2 are wisdom, understanding, and counsel. The key is to be guided by the Spirit of God.

Romans 8:14 (NASB) *"For all who are being led by the Spirit of God, these are sons of God."*

The key to the processes of God is submission.

No Submission, then No Remission

God is a God of the increase. He is always bringing us to a place of increase. Let the spirit of God be our guide, and He will show us our way, for He is the way, and we will begin to bring the future and our destiny into the present.

See the new image of you, and you will be.

Are our patterns changing? Are we growing?

There is no growth without change. There is either forward movement and change, or you will begin to move backward. Submit to the processes of God, and see Him bring you deeper, wider and higher.

That speaks of dimension. That speaks of more volume of Christ. As you enter into new dimensions, you will see the image of the new you and it will be more like Christ.

Break Out to Break In

I am somewhere in the future, and I look a lot better than I do right now. I hear the Holy Spirit say "break out to break in." Break out of the former things and break into the new things.

Isaiah 43:18-19 (AMPC) *"Do not [earnestly] remember the former things; neither consider the things of old. Behold, I am doing a new thing! Now it springs forth; do you not perceive and know it and will you not heed to it? I will even make a way in the wilderness and rivers in the desert."*

We have a lot of churches in the desert. God can provide new life if we will move out of the former things.

Begin to submit and see your future pulled into the present. Submit to God's process.

CHAPTER SEVEN

THE FULFILLMENT OF THE PROCESS

When we are in the spirit, we enter into a new dimension. In the spirit, we see and hear different things. We begin to operate with our five senses and the gifts of the spirit.

Our five natural senses can operate in the spirit and be spiritual senses. We can see, hear, smell, taste, and feel in the spirit realm. All spiritual senses can see.

We are operating out of the spirit and not the flesh or the old man. We are a new creation in Christ, and we are new men and women. We are not of this world but of another kingdom. We now belong to the kingdom of God. We can begin to see the future and begin to pull it into our present. We begin to sit in heavenly places and operate out of a higher and deeper place. We begin to look like the full-grown man of Christ.

Even Jesus went through a process. We don't know much about His life before twelve years old. Except we know He grew in wisdom and stature.

Luke 2:40 (AMPC) *"And the child grew and became strong in spirit, filled with wisdom; and the grace (favor and spiritual blessing) of God was upon Him."*

He was learning how to engage with mankind. He was a good son that was going through the process as He matured. That sounds like what we should do. He learned what everyday life was like and what one would experience growing up with hurts and the pain along with the enjoyment of life as a boy. We think of the man Jesus at thirty-three, but what about the boy at six and ten.

He could see the future and knew His purpose that was released before the foundation of the earth. God the father looked into the future and laid Jesus' purpose out. He gives us examples of how to see the future and to begin to bring it into the present. As we do this, we can start to see the full-grown man of Christ develop within us.

Jesus in His process as a young boy was learning to communicate and learn what the Father's heart desired. At the age of thirty-three, He was called the carpenter's son and could not do many works in His own town. The people of His home town could not see the future, because they were looking in the past and present.

The Old Has a Strong Hold

I realize the OLD has a strong HOLD. We will not realize how much of a hold the old has until we begin to move into the new and that which is ahead of us. This is a new revelation for me and I will continually seek that which is ahead. I have been shaking off old religious ways for way too long. We have to operate from being in His presence and not from our own performance, just as Jesus moved from what He heard and saw the Father do and say.

His yoke is easy and His burden light.

Matthew 11:30 (AMPC) *"For My yoke is wholesome (useful, good-not harsh, hard, sharp, or pressing, but comfortable, gracious, and pleasant), and My burden is light and easy to be borne."*

The yoke is the anointing or presence of Christ. We cannot experience the yoke, His yoke that is easy, until we have taken it on us and died to the old man and substituted our performance for His presence.

His ways and thoughts have to become ours. There are some old religious mindsets that have said you could only have one or two of the gifts of the spirit if any at all. We can have all that Christ has for us.

The old restricts and the new sets us free. The old religious wine says it is better. It has a better way. It says we are better and don't need any change, we have arrived and attained what we need. It says we know what God wants to do and how He wants to do it.

God deliver us!

The old will always settle for the good and miss God's best. The old will always operate out of the way it always has. If we are not functioning from being in His presence then we are operating out of the old, our own reasoning, and our performance-based mindsets. That has been the way we have been doing it and how many still do.

Acts 17:28a (AMPC) *"For in Him we live and move and have our being;"*

God is changing the way we move and have our being.

We will never leave the old until we taste the new wine and only then will we say the latter and that which was saved for last is better. We have always thought the best was now and not in the future. Only when we get the new taste of the new wine, the new attitude and the new position of a living sacrifice, will we begin to move into a higher place and begin to sit in heavenly places.

Philippians 3:13-15 (AMPC) *"I do not consider, brethren, that I have captured and made it my own (yet), but thing I do {it is one aspiration] forgetting what lies behind and straining forward to what is ahead. I press on toward the goal to win the [supreme and heavenly] prize to which God in Christ*

Jesus is calling us upward. So let those [of us] who are spiritually mature and full-grown hold these convictions; and if in any respect you have a different attitude of mind, God will make that clear to you also. "

Are you receiving this new attitude and position? When we do, we begin to move into the full nature of Christ and the anointed One begins to share His anointing with us. We begin to see the fulfillment of the processes. For there are many processes we go through. We are in Him and He is in us. His past, present, and future is in us. We can pull on all times. His past is written down and more of it can be revealed by the Holy Spirit. The present is with us and we can walk with Him every day. The future and the place He wants to bring us to is where we will be more like the full-grown Christ.

He said I am always with you. His purposes for us were laid out for us before the foundation of the earth and before we were even in our mother's womb. His purposes for us are past, present, and future.

Revelation 4:1 (AMPC) *"After this I looked and behold a door standing open in heaven! And the first voice which I had heard addressing me like [the calling of] a war trumpet said, Come up here, and I will show you what must take place in the future."*

God is not a respecter of persons and cannot lie. Let us continually pull our destiny from the future into the present.

What We See, We Can Be

I had a lady ask me how can you pull your future into the present. I immediately thought about something I had just received in a revelation. I told her that the Holy Spirit can give you a revelation and a new attitude or position, and though you have not experienced it, you can activate it and begin to operate in it.

I said I received the revelation that I can walk in the presence of God continually. Though I have not always walked in the presence of God by the Holy Spirit continually, I can begin to move into it. A new word or revelation can be now or in the future.

God sometimes gives me just one word, and I have to use it to move into the future. For me, some of the words have been "wait" and "more." Those words carry many meanings and activations for me.

The children of Israel saw the future but did not enter in and wandered around in circles for forty years until a whole generation passed away. However, a few took hold of it. Those few entered in and possessed the promised land. The future they acquired, they had seen in the past.

As we begin to move out of the old and into the new, we understand the heavy hold the old has on us. Even as we move out of the old religious order into the new kingdom's order, we will sometimes find ourselves leaning back on an old way. God will even honor that as long as we are seeking His heart.

We have to have our minds renewed every day so we can continually be moving higher, deeper, and wider into Christ and the fulfillment of Him and His processes for us in our future. When we do this, we begin to have the mind of Christ. We see all our attitudes and mindsets change as we become living sacrifices.

The old is gone and everything is new. We begin to move in a new dimension.

Isaiah 43:18-19 (AMPC) *"Behold, I am doing a new thing! Now it springs forth; do you not perceive and know it and will you not give head to it? I will even make a way into the wilderness and rivers in the desert"*

A lot of churches have dried up, but God can bring the Holy Spirit to water them again.

The old way of ministering will become less effective as we move into the new era that is on the way. There is a continual process of moving into the fulfillment of the processes and the full-grown Christ. We learn to see in the future and pull it into our present. We keep moving into that which is ahead.

If your ministry gets stale and frustrating, you might want to look for a new way of ministering and a renewed relationship with the Lord. That which is ahead and new is not the same way we have been doing things.

The Status Quo Must Go

The Old Must Lose Its Hold

The church will look a whole lot different in the future. A new era, a new age is approaching. Begin to pull the future into your present and see the full-grown Christ begin to form in you. You then will see the fulfillment of the processes of God take hold.

The season we are moving into is a season of acceleration, influence and expectation. What I hear is this: We are not in a Volkswagen or a Mustang but a 6 speed semi-automatic Ferrari. A very fast accelerating car. We will shift gears into higher levels and some already have, then we will go into automatic drive. In automatic drive, we begin to settle into the shifts that we already have and begin to understand the revelations that we have received in those shifts. We begin to settle into an acceleration process. When we settle in, we begin to actively participate in the process.

We have to be positioned in our proper seat to experience the new speed that we are going. We are moving into new places we have never been, mysteries and revelations that have never been revealed before are beginning to open up faster and at a larger place.

What used to take months or years to move into, can now be moved into in hours or days.

God, by the Holy Spirit, is bringing us into a new place where the full-grown, mature Christ is formed in us and the fulfillment of the processes of God takes hold.

Father, help us be positioned to receive the new place that you want to bring us to. Holy Spirit, help our minds be renewed to have a new mindset and not let our old mindsets hold us back. Give us the mind of Christ. Let us see the future and begin to pull the new into the present. Let us begin to become the fully mature Christ that is in us. Amen.

THE ARMY OF GOD

by Gerald Courtney

I hear a sound in the heavens.

It's the sound of war.

I hear the feet of many coming

from near and far.

It's time for battle.

It's time for war.

It's not with flesh and blood.

But with powers above.

The church is being realigned.

The church is being redesigned.

The people of God are an army.

Each and every one.

So get on your armor.

Get ready to fight.

Because we have to set the enemy to flight.

The battle is not with hands.

But with the Lord's plans.

Only in prayer can we go.

Only in prayer will we know.

Dedication is called for.

A sound is in the heavens.

The sound of a trumpet.

The sound of war.

I hear a sound in the heavens.

I hear a sound of war.

I hear the feet of many,

Coming from near and far.

It's time for battle.

It's time for war.

ACKNOWLEDGMENTS

I thank God for the revelation that He gives me to increase my life in Him. I want to thank Teacher Susan Barnett, author of *As One*, for the first and last edit of this book. I want to thank inspirational author Deborah Lynne (author-deborahlynne.com) for an additional edit and all her help of setting up this book. I want to thank my daughter-in-law Kharis Courtney (khariscreations.com) for helping design the cover and all her excellent work, along with my son Jordan Courtney for editing and formatting this book. I want to thank all my friends that kept telling me you must publish this book. I want to thank Prophet Anton La Grange that prophesied this book would come to reality. I want to thank my dad who said finish what you start and the legacy he left behind. I want to thank Apostle Mike Barnett for his invaluable impartation into my life.

NOTES

Made in the USA
Columbia, SC
14 May 2025